Images of Modern America

CLEVELAND'S ROCK AND ROLL VENUES

Front Cover: The band Abbey Rodeo (a take on the Beatles album *Abbey Road*) formed in 2000. While it has had various members through the years, the band has kept its commitment to "play a variety of songs people know, along with original music." This has brought them local acclaim and hundreds of regular gigs. This photograph was taken in 2017, when Abbey Rodeo performed at the new, state-of-the-art Mentor Civic Amphitheater for the "Mentor Rocks" series. The members who performed at this show include PJ Philips (keyboard, vocals; not pictured on cover), Bob Yocum (guitar, fiddle, vocals; not pictured on cover), Jim Bonfanti (drums, vocals), Verne McClelland (guitar, vocals), Larry Kadlub (bass, vocals), and Chris Butcher (guitar, vocals; not pictured on cover). (Photograph by Jeff Hace; see page 88.)

Upper Back Cover: Blondie at Little Theater. (Photograph by Janet Macoska; see page 19.)

Lower Back Cover (from left to right): Public Hall (Photograph by Janet Macoska; see page 17), Music Box Supper Club (Photograph by Marla Zwinggi; see page 7), East Shore Park (Photograph by Jeff Hace; see page 71).

Images of Modern America

CLEVELAND'S ROCK AND ROLL VENUES

Deanna R. Adams
Foreword by Janet Macoska

ARCADIA PUBLISHING

ISBN 978-1-4671-0446-3

Published by Arcadia Publishing
Charleston, South Carolina

Printed in the United States of America

Library of Congress Control Number: 2019947577

For all general information, please contact Arcadia Publishing:
Telephone 843-853-2070
Fax 843-853-0044
E-mail sales@arcadiapublishing.com
For customer service and orders:
Toll-Free 1-888-313-2665

Visit us on the Internet at www.arcadiapublishing.com

It is only fitting that I dedicate this book to my friend Janet Macoska, whose rocking photographs enhance this book. A mere thank you is not enough, but it is certainly genuine. Cleveland is lucky to have you. And so am I. (Photograph by Jean Schnell.)

Contents

FOREWORD

Music finds you in many ways. When I was five years old, I had a crush on cute young singing star Ricky Nelson, who performed weekly on his family's television show, *The Adventures of Ozzie and Harriet*. By age 10, my world was rocked—as many were—by those four mop tops from Liverpool, the Beatles. The Beatles coming to America got me hooked on their music, along with all the pop and rock music that quickly followed. I felt a great need to be a part of that. But since I had no talent in making the music, I found my entrée into that world via writing and photography. My first photograph was published when I was 12; it was of Sonny and Cher talking to fans on Big Jack Armstrong's radio show on AM station WKYC. *Teen Screen* magazine published it in 1967. Payment was $2.

With that, I was off and clicking into my lifelong career. By 1974, I was a professional rock and roll photographer. You might ask if I'd seen the inside of every music club, bar, college gym, or theater, and the answer is not necessarily, though there were many.

If you were attending concerts in Northeast Ohio in the 1960s, those shows were most likely at the Cleveland Music Hall or its big brother, Cleveland Public Hall. Late in the 1960s, Blossom Music Center opened, followed by the Richfield Coliseum, which held more than 20,000 patrons. The Cleveland Municipal Stadium, normally used for the city's football and baseball teams, became the granddaddy of all Cleveland concert experiences in the 1970s with the World Series of Rock concerts presented by Belkin Productions. The city rented out the 80,000-seat outdoor stadium for these events, which usually featured five top bands playing music during events that lasted from noon until midnight.

These were our mini-Woodstock experiences, with audiences camping out on the field, shrouding themselves with tarps and plastic when the weather turned wet or succumbing to sunstroke in the blazing sun. The roster of talent was stunning.

While you, the reader, have your own memories of the concert venues and clubs that came and went with the times, my memories are not the same as yours. My interests were the bands on stage and getting the opportunity to take great photographs. That meant having good lighting and not bothering the audience members who paid money to get into the venue to see their favorite acts.

Throughout the 1970s and into the 1980s, I spent every Monday and Tuesday night at the Cleveland Agora because that club featured many national acts. Audience members spent the day waiting in line for the doors to open so they could stake their claim to a good spot in front of the stage, and I needed to—diplomatically and courteously—get in front of these rabid fans. I did so by talking to some of these fans before the show. I explained that I needed to be in front for a short while and asked for their understanding and help. In exchange, I'd send them some photographs. In those days, with no digital photographs or e-mail, I'd make extra prints and send them out. I can't attest to what other photographers did, but I had these brothers and sisters willingly looking out for me up there!

My main circuit for concerts was the Richfield Coliseum, Blossom Music Center, Agora, Front Row Theater, and some of the Playhouse Square theaters, especially the Allen Theatre, which became a great rock and roll hall—low stage, great lights, and wild crowd. All of these venues had good-to-great lighting, as you'd expect with the caliber of talent they featured. The Front Row Theater was special, as it had its stage in the center of a circle of seats, and the talent spun around (s…l…o…w…l…y) throughout the performance. So, it was quite the challenge to get the artist in the spotlight, click off a few frames, and wait for them to spin a full circle before you got another shot.

Most recently, the Tower City Amphitheater and Nautica have proven to be well-run venues in the Flats that are fun to photograph and easy to get out of once you're finished with the three-song shoot, which is now standard for photographers.

During the past five years, I have been the house photographer at the Hard Rock Rocksino LIVE venue (now the MGM Center Stage) and have found it to be a wonderful venue. Our lighting guy, John, is awesome and creative, so my three-song limit is not the curse it's often been. I've never shot better.

This book gives a detailed look at the unique music venues of our town, so join Deanna Adams as she shines the spotlight on the Cleveland area's finest concert venues. She has the stories, and I contributed many of the photographs. We make a great team! Rock on!

—Janet Macoska, 2019

ACKNOWLEDGMENTS

This book would not exist without the talent and generosity of so many people. It was fun to look through all the images but so hard to choose the ones that best represent the venues that gave us all so many memories then and now. First, a huge thank you and hugs go to photographers Janet Macoska and Jeff Hace—true professionals whose enthusiasm, time, and effort, along with their willingness to share their talented work, have made this book what it is. I am so grateful and honored to call them friends.

Others who greatly contributed to this book, whether via images or information, include Bear Jackson, George Shuba, Ricky Benninger, Mike Miller, Rick Novario, Dolores Resch, Drew Losch, Nancy Yovan, John C. Benson, Dan Cornelius, Cindy Barber, Mark Leddy, Nathan Rogers, Joe Kleon, Kevin McCann, Tim Roush, Kendall Stauffer, Kay Bryson, Judie Vegh, Bill "DJ Hunter" Harpst, Kira Lugo, Aprell Burkey, Joe Milliken, Louis Haas, Steffi Wegewitz, Tammi Hansen, Marla Zwinggi, Keith Marlowe, Mike Tata, Gene Schwartz, Gene Taylor, Jason Hanley, Greg Drugan, Al Kaston, and—of course—my husband, Jeffrey Adams, for his contributed photograph and his always unwavering support.

Introduction

As anyone familiar with rock and roll music knows by now, Cleveland has been an integral part of this scene literally from day one, beginning with Alan Freed, the famed disc jockey who began playing R&B records and calling it rock and roll. He also hosted what is now referred to as the first-ever rock and roll concert, which took place at the Cleveland Arena on March 21, 1952.

My books *Rock 'n' Roll and the Cleveland Connection*, published by Kent State University Press, and *Cleveland's Rock and Roll Roots*, published by Arcadia Publishing, have documented this history well, I believe.

So, why another book chronicling this topic, and why one that solely focuses on the music venues of the Greater Cleveland area? First, the former title was published twenty years ago, and a lot of clubs and venues have rocked the city since then. The latter title, now ten years old, could not cover it all, despite a full chapter on clubs and venues.

If you have spent any time in the Cleveland area, you know where I am coming from. There have always been great places to enjoy live music any night of the week in Cleveland—so many places, in fact, that I could not possibly include all of them in this book. This is one of the many reasons Cleveland is the designated home of the Rock & Roll Hall of Fame and Museum.

The lifeline of this music is as ever-winding as the Cuyahoga River and runs through the heart and soul of the North Coast. This book should interest all generations. Baby boomers will enjoy reminiscing about the clubs they used to frequent, basking in the images that spark so many fond memories. The younger generation will have fun seeing vintage photographs of the clubs they missed out on along with images of their current favorite musical stomping grounds, all while learning about how these nightspots came to be and the artists who have played at them.

Because of space limitations, I was unable to tell the complete story behind some of these images. For those interested, I refer readers to the more in-depth *Rock 'n' Roll and the Cleveland Connection*. I also regret that I could not fit in every venue this great rock town has to offer. For that, I simply suggest Google, because in Cleveland, there is no shortage of entertainment.

I am excited that this book will be a great companion to my other Arcadia Publishing book, *Cleveland's Rock and Roll Roots*, as it is not just a celebration of this area's venues but also honors the musicians who make the music that has absolutely become the soundtrack of our lives.

While some may question rock's continued relevance, there is no denying the breadth of its influence. Rock and roll is a large, hearty branch on a very old, robust tree, and it will never die—especially not in Cleveland.

So, yes, here is another Cleveland rock book that you, your parents, your children, and even your grandchildren are going to love. Let us celebrate Cleveland's great music scene once again!

*Note to reader: Every attempt was made to find the original photographer of each photograph in this book. Please let me know if there is an oversight, and it will be corrected in the second printing.

One

The Early Concert Venues

One simply cannot begin a book on Cleveland's rock and roll venues without starting with the Cleveland Arena. Located at 3717 Euclid Avenue, this facility originally hosted sporting events, such as ice hockey games for the Cleveland Barons. Then, on March 21, 1952, WJW deejay Alan Freed put on a rocking event, the Moondog Coronation Ball, that became the first of its kind.

Although that concert was by no means a success, other venues, including the Playhouse Square theater venues, got on the rock bandwagon and began hosting popular rock and pop acts in the 1960s. This set a precedent for club owners to bring rock and roll to the masses. Cleveland had the venues and the rabid fans, which soon led to the city becoming known as the Rock and Roll Capital of the World.

MOONDOG CORONATION BALL AT THE CLEVELAND ARENA. Alan Freed thought this 10,000-seat venue was perfect for his grand show, but when more than 20,000 fans showed up, it quickly became chaotic, and fire marshals shut down the concert before the first act had finished. The event became front-page news, and rock and roll history instantly earned—in the words of Joan Jett—a "bad reputation." (Photograph by Peter Hastings; courtesy of Gloria Hastings.)

THE ARENA, ELVIS POSTER. Elvis played the Cleveland Arena in 1956, just as he was becoming a major star with "Heartbreak Hotel." But this was not his first visit north of the Mason-Dixon Line. That came in February 1955, when he played Cleveland's Circle Theater; he also played that fall at Brooklyn High School and St. Michael's Hall. By the time another year had passed, Elvis was indeed the king, and his skyrocketing career had earned him arena status. (Courtesy of Bear at Raw Sugar Art Studios.)

THE BEATLES AT THE CLEVELAND PUBLIC AUDITORIUM. While the arena kick-started the city's rock and roll movement, Cleveland's Public Auditorium, also known as Public Hall, located at 500 Lakeside Avenue, kept the momentum going in 1964 with the most anticipated concert in rock history. Although there were other pop acts on the bill, it was obvious from the first scream that fans were there to see the four "mop tops." The band was on a wild ride that included becoming the first musical act in history to occupy Billboard's top five chart positions in a single week. (Courtesy of Bear at Raw Sugar Art Studios.)

Public Hall. In 1964, pop radio stations WHK and KYW furiously fought to secure sponsorship for the Beatles' first U.S. tour stop in Cleveland. When WHK snagged it after some clever behind-the-scenes maneuvering, the station became the "official Beatles radio station." The Beatles sat down for a press conference before the Public Hall concert, and it all went smoothly—but this was not so at the concert itself. A herd of overzealous fans rushed the stage despite the line of stern-looking policemen attempting to keep them at bay, causing a 10-minute delay. The same thing happened when the Rolling Stones performed soon after, which led to Public Hall's "Beatles ban," which prohibited major rock bands from performing at the venue—for a time. (Both, courtesy of George Shuba Photography.)

Creedence Clearwater Revival and the Who Posters. The Beatles ban was lifted in the summer of 1966, and Public Hall once again became the go-to place for concerts. The decade ended with the venue hosting an impressive list of rock acts, including the Jimi Hendrix Experience, the Doors, the Grateful Dead, and Creedence Clearwater Revival (CCR). Included on the CCR bill was local band Silk, best known as one of "Cleveland's Favorite Son" Michael Stanley's early rock groups. The Who jump-started the 1970s with its Public Hall performance, and in 1972, David Bowie and his Spiders from Mars made their historic U.S. debut. (Both, courtesy of Bear at Raw Sugar Art Studios.)

Grand Funk Railroad, Mark Farner. The 1970s saw nearly every rock act perform at Public Hall. Grand Funk Railroad already had a large following in Cleveland, but when the band opened for Led Zeppelin, they took over the place, playing hits like "Time Machine" and "I'm Your Captain (Closer to Home)." According to many who were there, Led Zeppelin was not at its best (rumors of too much partying), and after some booing, Zeppelin left the stage, and Grand Funk returned for an additional set with a shirtless Mark Farner, who thrilled female fans. This concert alone proved that no matter how big the act, Cleveland fans expect nothing but the best when it comes to rock and roll. (Photograph by Janet Macoska.)

Public Hall Inductions. Through the years, the Cleveland Public Auditorium has played host to thousands of rock and roll acts, so it is fitting that this large historic and beloved venue hosted the ceremony for the Rock & Roll Hall of Fame (a.k.a. the Rock Hall) inductions. The first inductions to take place in Cleveland happened on May 6, 1997, a year and a half after the ceremonious opening of the Rock Hall. It took a while for the ceremony to return, but return it did—in 2009, 2012, 2015, and 2018. It is now held at this venue every other year. Fans look forward to 2020, when the party will once again continue in Cleveland. (Both, photograph by Janet Macoska.)

Music Hall. There are two venues located inside the Cleveland Public Auditorium for smaller performances: the 3,000-seat Music Hall and the 600-seat Little Theater. Music Hall offers fans a closer look at the stars, and people especially enjoy seeing hometown rockers, such as Eric Carmen, perform there. Carmen made his name with the power pop group the Raspberries, which formed in Cleveland and had national hits like "Go All the Way" and "I Wanna Be with You." The band broke up in 1975, and Carmen began his solo career, which gave him more success with his biggest hit, "All by Myself," a song that has been covered by a number of recording artists, including Céline Dion, who took it to even greater international acclaim. (Photograph by Janet Macoska.)

BLONDIE. New wave band Blondie, featuring Debbie Harry, performed at Public Hall's smallest venue, Little Theater, in 1978, headlining a Cleveland show for the first time. Blondie soon captured much larger audiences with No. 1 hits "The Tide Is High" and "Rapture." The group was inducted into the Rock & Roll Hall of Fame in 2006. (Photograph by Janet Macoska.)

U2. U2, featuring lead singer Bono, played the Music Hall in May 1983 during the band's *War* Tour. Fans appreciated being up close in this intimate setting. U2 returned to the hall in December 1984 to support its new album, *The Unforgettable Fire*. The group was inducted into the Rock Hall in 2005, which was the first year it was eligible. (Photograph by Janet Macoska.)

Musicarnival Posters. While Musicarnival, in Warrensville Heights, was certainly not known as a rock and roll venue (it was more the circus tent/theater variety), it made Cleveland rock history with a notable concert: Led Zeppelin's first visit to the city. The opener was Cleveland group the James Gang. (Unfortunately, the band is not mentioned on these posters.) Note the date of the show—July 20, 1969, the night of the Apollo 11's historic moon landing. After the well-received concert, band members hung out to watch the first man walk on the moon. That night included one giant leap for mankind and another great step for rock and roll. (Both, courtesy of Bear at Raw Sugar Art Studios.)

Hullabaloo Clubs. While most venues catered to adults, there were a few clubs that welcomed younger crowds and gave them memorable experiences. The Hullabaloo clubs were named after the musical variety show that ran for just one year, from January 1965 to April 1966. These Northeast Ohio venues lasted a bit longer than the show, but not by much. They were not fancy on the outside, but inside, the clubs showcased many rock stars just beginning their careers. Fans got to see up-and-comers like Rod Stewart, Todd Rundgren, and Alice Cooper, with local bands as openers. The James Gang (when the group included five members) shared the stage with the Yardbirds in 1968. Poster designer Bear Jackson calls the image at right "one of the most beautiful concert posters we ever created." (Above, courtesy of Drew Losch Collection; right, courtesy of Bear at Raw Sugar Art Studios.)

ALLEN THEATRE MARQUEES. The Allen Theatre, in Playhouse Square, welcomed rock groups early on. In the 1960s, many concerts held there featured acts like the Yardbirds, Cream, the Byrds, and Santana. In the 1970s came the Grateful Dead, Pink Floyd, and, in 1975, Bruce Springsteen. That same year, the Sensational Alex Harvey Band, a Scottish hard-glam group, headlined the Allen thanks to frequent airplay on radio station WMMS and a successful concert at the Agora in 1974. Opening for the band was a local group from the Canton area formed by drummer Joe Vitale. Vitale often played and recorded with other musicians, including Joe Walsh, Michael Stanley, and Crosby, Stills & Nash, among others. When popular acts like Genesis were scheduled to perform, the lines got long, and the line became a party in itself, with kids chatting excitedly in anticipation for the music that awaited them. (Both, photograph by Janet Macoska.)

Allen Theatre. The Playhouse Square theaters offered the perfect setup for rock bands, with a big stage, lots of seats, and a sophisticated atmosphere that—for the most part—kept attendees on good behavior. The acts could also be more dramatic during their shows. Genesis, featuring lead singer Peter Gabriel, was known for theatrical performances. In this photograph taken at the Allen in 1974, Gabriel performs "Watcher of the Skies" while dressed in a cape with bat wings and dramatic makeup. (Photograph by Janet Macoska.)

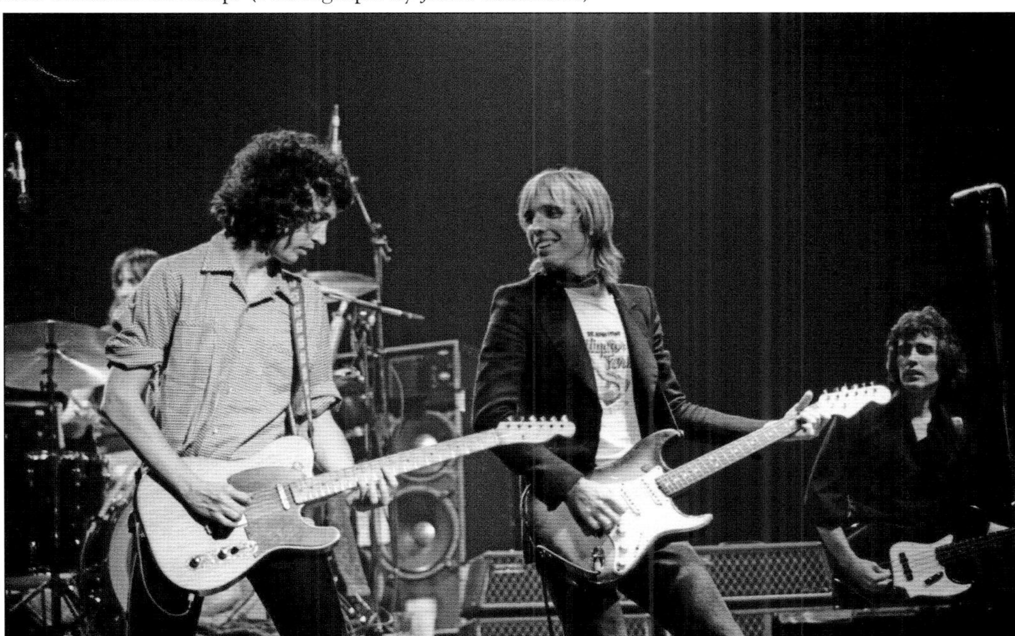

Palace Theater. With a seating capacity of over 3,000, the Palace Theater was large enough to showcase big productions and, of course, big rock acts. Here, Tom Petty plays the Palace early in his career, November 1979, in support of his *Damn the Torpedoes* album. Although the seating capacity went down to 2,714 after a $36.4 million renovation project in 1988, the Palace Theater (now the Connor Palace) still boasted the second-largest theater in Playhouse Square, with the State Theatre being the largest. (Photograph by Janet Macoska.)

State Theatre. Like its neighbors in Playhouse Square, the State Theatre (now Keybank State Theatre), was one of the most prestigious places for musicians to play and hosted numerous musical acts. These two photographs demonstrate the diversity of talent that Cleveland venues have always offered. Although Smokey Robinson (left) was not considered a "rock" act, he was certainly a major player on the extended branch that was Motown. Smokey Robinson and the Miracles gave the Motown label its first No. 1 hit, "Shop Around," which was followed by many more hits for the label. On November 15, 2008, the State hosted a tribute to well-respected musician Les Paul. Like others who performed that night, Slash, of Guns N' Roses, was proud to hang backstage with his guitar hero, as shown below. (Both, photograph by Janet Macoska.)

Two

The World-Famous Cleveland Agora

In 1966, Henry "Hank" LoConti opened the Agora, a true rock club for those who were age 18 and over, near Case Western Reserve University. However, it quickly outgrew the 200-capacity venue. LoConti found a new building within a year, moving to East Twenty-fourth Street, closer to Cleveland State University. Here was a place baby boomers could hang out with each other while listening to their favorite local, regional, and national bands. Even the basement saw rock action amid its several name changes—from the Viking's Den to the Mistake and the Pop Shop.

Throughout the 1970s, LoConti opened a number of Agora clubs across the nation, but most agree that the Cleveland club was special. In 1984, the club closed due to a fire, but the rock entrepreneur soon found another fitting place for his beloved club at 5000 Euclid Avenue. Today, the beautifully restored and updated century-old building contains a 2,000-capacity theater, which is now used for more than just rock events, and a 600-capacity ballroom with a more intimate atmosphere. LoConti passed away in 2014, but his vision and venerable clubs live on so that future generations can continue to rock.

Agora Jukebox. Like so many Cleveland rock fans, graphic artist, designer, illustrator, and musician Rick Novario grew up with great music on the North Coast. "What excited me about designing 'Hank' on the jukebox is that I knew he was once a jukebox vendor," Novario said. "And I wanted to honor the bands that inspired me when I'd see them at all the clubs, especially at the Agora. So I had to include American Noise, Wild Horses, Love Affair, and Beau Coup, just to name a few." For hometown musicians, performing at the Agora was the crème de la crème, and LoConti always provided an opportunity. The Agora featured "Golden Sundays," a "Coffee Break Concert" on Wednesdays, and the biggest draw of all was unusual for a club—"Monday Nights Out at the Agora." This ever-popular rock venue delivered a different musical experience every night for both musicians and fans, who came to hear their favorite music or check out something new. (Courtesy of Rick Novario collection.)

The Police. While the Cleveland Agora was king, there were other Agora venues as well; at one time, there were 13 throughout the United States. Each one offered the best in current music, with many acts performing at one of these clubs during their first visit to the United States, including the Police, who headlined the Painesville Agora, located 30 miles east of Cleveland, in March 1979. Opening band the Romantics, a power pop/new wave act from Detroit, had just released its hit, "What I Like About You." (Courtesy of Bear at Raw Sugar Art Studios.)

Agora Marquee. When the Agora moved to its current location in the mid-1980s, the revered club needed a you-can't-miss-it marquee to announce the new era. The building already had a rich Cleveland rock history, as it was the former WHK Auditorium, home of WHK-AM, which hosted many of the radio station's concerts. It was briefly known as the Cleveland Grande Ballroom in the late 1960s and became home to WMMS-FM from 1968 to 1975. The Agora's hot-pink neon sign needed repairs when its current management, AEG Presents, LLC, took over. So, the iconic marquee got a face-lift in 2018—along with the spacious theater, the ballroom, the club's three bars, and the bathrooms, of course—for a cost of $3 million. Today, this venue is available not just for rock shows but also a number of other events. (Left, photograph by Janet Macoska; below, photograph by Judie Vegh.)

Agora, Then and Now. From the beginning, the Agora brought in acts of all types, even if they were not favorites of the rock majority. In the 1970s, there were some seminal punk/alternative bands that were not embraced by media or concert promoters. However, the Velvet Underground, with lead singer and guitarist Lou Reed, found a friend not only in the Agora but also in *Plain Dealer* rock reporter Jane Scott. As a result, Reed, pictured above (at left) in 1974, often played in Cleveland. True to form, the Agora continues this legacy, catering to a new generation of musicians—no matter what the genre. In March 2018, hard-rock band Michael Schenker Group (MSG), consisting of former members of the Scorpions and UFO guitarist Michael Schenker, gave a performance in the Agora Theatre that fans are sure to remember. (Both, photograph by Janet Macoska.)

Ben Orr at the Mistake. This venue, originally called the Viking's Den, was located in the basement of the Agora. It was a hot spot for those hungry for the more alternative sounds of the day, such as blues, reggae, and new wave/punk. This made it the perfect place for the Cars to perform in 1978. Although the band formed in Boston, it consisted of two former Clevelanders—Ric Ocasek, who once lived in Maple Heights, and the much-adored Benjamin Orr, whose star was launched early on the North Coast. The band's self-titled debut album sold six million copies, and the Cars earned a "Best New Artist" designation from Rolling Stone that same year. (Photograph by Janet Macoska.)

The Pop Shop. The Mistake turned into the Pop Shop in 1983 and continued to serve up a smorgasbord of diverse rock and roll, as indicated by the waiting crowd shown here. In July of that year, the monthly calendar included local and national acts, such as the Cramps, Stiv Bators, Wild Giraffes, the Generators, and the News (featuring former Raspberries guitarist Wally Bryson); all of these acts consisted of current or former Clevelanders. (Photograph by Linda Woods.)

Glass Harp. On March 22, 2013, the Agora hosted a special event honoring its founder, Hank LoConti. Many Cleveland musicians, fans, friends, and members of the media gathered to pay their respects, even giving LoConti his own throne on stage as they paid tribute to him. In attendance were members of Glass Harp, a progressive-rock trio that has a notable Cleveland history. This gave photographer Janet Macoska an opportunity, and she snapped this pictured of Glass Harp in the old Agora dressing room as they leaned against the iconic brick wall where many performing musicians have signed their names. (Photograph by Janet Macoska.)

Agora Theatre. Today, the new Agora endures by presenting diverse musical acts as rock music continues to evolve. Agora fans often attend shows that have a harder edge—think heavy metal, rap, punk, and metalcore—such as Killswitch Engage (KSG). The group's Agora performance in November 2018 easily filled the large venue with enthusiastic fans. "I remember once playing the Agora with a little-known band called Caveman," KSG bassist Mike D'Antonio told *News-Herald* reporter John Benson. "Cleveland has always been spastic as far as crowd response." That kind of response is perfect for concert photographers like Nathan Rogers, who is often on hand to capture moments like this. (Photograph by Nathan Rogers.)

Preserving LoConti's Vision. Whereas the Agora used to be a gritty, eclectic music venue run by one man, his family, and a few trusted associates, the 21st-century Agora is owned by a major entertainment corporation, AEG Presents. Fortunately, the company honored the Agora's cherished history and has maintained LoConti's vision. Despite a multimillion-dollar renovation, AEG Presents managed to combine the building's vintage charm with state-of-the-art brilliance, giving Clevelanders a venue they can enjoy for decades to come. (Photograph by Judie Vegh.)

Three

THE BIG-TIME VENUES

During the 1970s, Cleveland's hottest venues were Swingos, the Cleveland Municipal Stadium, and the Richfield Coliseum. Swingos Celebrity Hotel, located at 1800 Euclid Avenue, became the inspiration for the movie *Almost Famous* due to its national reputation for wild and loose rock and roll parties. Named after its owner, Jim Swingos, this legendary restaurant/bar/hotel gave stars the license to do whatever they wanted—and they did.

The Cleveland Municipal Stadium, the old home of the Browns and Indians, played host to Saturday afternoon World Series of Rock concerts for six straight summers.

The Coliseum, located in Richfield, Ohio, was a sports arena built to replace the Cleveland Arena, but thanks to Jules and Mike Belkin of Belkin Productions, it also became a favorite place to catch a rock concert. This electrifying musical era was a great time to be a young rocker in Cleveland.

Swingos. Rock stars knew they "made it" when they saw their name on the prestigious listing of celebrities posted in the renowned Swingos lobby. In the photograph at left, Fee Waybill looks like a typical 1970s guy. But on stage, he fronted the glam-rock band the Tubes, known for shock rock theatrics. Waybill's onstage character, Quay Lube, wore a blonde fright wig and platform boots, and the band's hit song, "White Punks on Dope," became an anthem. Waybill and his band performed at the Allen Theatre in 1975, then, like so many, stayed at Swingos, where he proudly pointed out that he was in good company. (Both, photograph by Janet Macoska.)

A Party Place. Swingos's lounge bar was the perfect party spot and the place to be seen. During a booking at Public Hall in 1982, Prince's protégé Denise "Vanity" Matthews (left), lead singer of the 1980s girl group Vanity 6, partied with another Prince acquaintance, Morris Day, funk/R&B singer of the Time. While Swingos was often known for its decadence, guests dressed up to show off their glamour and revel in style at the club. (Photograph by Janet Macoska.)

Kid Leo at Swingos. Anything went at Swingos, and one never knew who he or she might see there. Fans could stop in and spot a variety of actors, singers, and even presidents (Jimmy Carter). Kid Leo, perhaps the most popular of all the revered WMMS deejays, was a regular. He mingled with more than just rock stars and is pictured here in 1979 with country star Charlie "Devil Went Down to Georgia" Daniels (right), who was in town to play at the Music Hall. (Photograph by Janet Macoska.)

CONCERT CROWDS. The first rock concert at the Cleveland Stadium was the Beatles in 1966. In 1974, venue owners Jules and Mike orchestrated what became the city's biggest outdoor summer event from 1974 through 1980. The World Series of Rock kicked off in fine style on June 23, 1974, with Lynyrd Skynyrd, Joe Walsh and Barnstorm, REO Speedwagon, and the Beach Boys. It was quite a lineup—and one that appealed to a diverse group of fans. Those fans waited patiently outside the venue for the gates to open. After they moved inside, they continued the party until long after dark. (Both, courtesy of Cleveland Press Collection.)

STADIUM SECURITY. With crowds at a Cleveland Stadium concert numbering anywhere from 40,000 to more than 80,000, heavy security was always on hand, as shown above at an August 1977 performance by Peter Frampton at the peak of his career. In 1974, the venue's debut year, Crosby, Stills & Nash headlined a concert that drew 81,000. In 1978, the Rolling Stones surpassed that record with 82,500 fans. These numbers are no surprise considering the huge talents fans could see by paying between $8 and $12.50 for a ticket. (Photograph by Janet Macoska.)

WORLD SERIES POSTER. Even with beefed-up security and a hospital tent staffed with doctors and nurses, there were enough disturbing incidents and chaotic events that they ultimately led to the end of the World Series of Rock in 1980. But, in true rock style, its final lineup was one that was not to be missed. Although the series ended, the stadium still continued to host concerts until the historic venue was demolished in November 1996 after the Browns hightailed it to Baltimore and the city realized that this storied building would need enormous repairs. (Courtesy of Bear at Raw Sugar Art Studios.)

Bruce at the Stadium. Since his debut concert at the Allen Theatre in 1974, Bruce Springsteen was a staple on the Cleveland music scene, returning during each concert tour. He played a sold-out show at the stadium in 1985, promoting his *Born in the U.S.A.* album and getting the crowd worked up—as always. True Cleveland Springsteen fans agree that his 1978 performance at the old East Twenty-fourth Street Agora during the celebration of the 10th anniversary of WMMS was the show never to be forgotten. (Photograph by Janet Macoska.)

Gladys Knight & the Pips. Throughout the 1980s, bands continued to rock the stadium in fine style. In 1983, fans enjoyed a real treat watching Gladys Knight & the Pips perform on a bill that included Aretha Franklin and the Temptations, all of whom had performed in the 1960s at another popular venue, Leo's Casino. The grand Cleveland Stadium, nicknamed "Lady on the Lake," enjoyed one last hoorah when it hosted the coveted Rock & Roll Hall of Fame concert in celebration of its 1995 opening. (Photograph by Janet Macoska.)

THE RICHFIELD COLISEUM. In 1974, the same year that the World Series of Rock began, an indoor coliseum opened in Richfield, Ohio, to replace the Cleveland Arena and house the Cleveland Cavaliers. This new arena also served as a musical palace for the next 20 years. Rock acts continually filled the 20,273-capacity venue. KISS was a favorite, performing there several times; here, lead singer Gene Simmons thrills the audience with what they came to see. (Photograph by Janet Macoska.)

Fleetwood Mac and George Harrison. Fleetwood Mac, always a Cleveland favorite, was riding high off its platinum-selling album, *Rumours*, when it performed to a packed audience at the Coliseum in 1977. If only it had gone that well for the highly anticipated George Harrison show set for December 1974. To fans' heartbreaking dismay, that day, a huge snowstorm hit Cleveland, and Harrison was forced to cancel. Worse yet, he was unable to reschedule and never came back to play in Cleveland. (Both, courtesy of Bear at Raw Sugar Art Studios.)

That's Entertainment. The Richfield Coliseum always hosted the best musical acts, starting with Frank Sinatra, who headlined during its debut opening in 1974. The large stage was visible from every seat, which Elton John fans appreciated when he performed there. On stage, there were great showmanship and entertaining acts, like John, and backstage was often the same—though a bit more playful. In 1978, Foghat members Dave Peverett and Rod Price decided to pass time with their own antics, as shown below. (Both, photograph by Janet Macoska.)

Legends at the Coliseum. When Michael Jackson and Queen first performed at the Coliseum, it was the peak of arena rock, and many of the musicians featured at the venue presented high-volume performances. In the 1977 image above, a young Freddie Mercury performs in his own unique style with Queen. At this time, the group had already scored one of its biggest hits, "Bohemian Rhapsody." In 1988, Michael Jackson performed at the Coliseum; this concert was to promote his latest album, *Bad*, which was released the previous year. (Both, photograph by Janet Macoska.)

Four

Downtown and Around Town

This chapter pays tribute to yesterday's venues that produced many memories for Clevelanders. While most are now long gone, there are a few that managed to either survive through the decades, such as the Flats' infamous Harbor Inn (open since the late 1800s) and the Cove in Geneva-on-the-Lake (open since 1963), or were closed for a time but then reopened, such as the Odeon. There were the dives in the "old Flats," such as D'Poos and Fagans, along with upscale restaurants like the Watermark and Sammy's.

Northeast Ohio—whether east side, west side, or south side—has never been short on taverns, restaurants, and nightclubs, and most have continually offered a diverse selection of musical acts that keep the city teeming with revelry—or, at least, amusement. The following chapter merely touches on a select few that are fondly remembered.

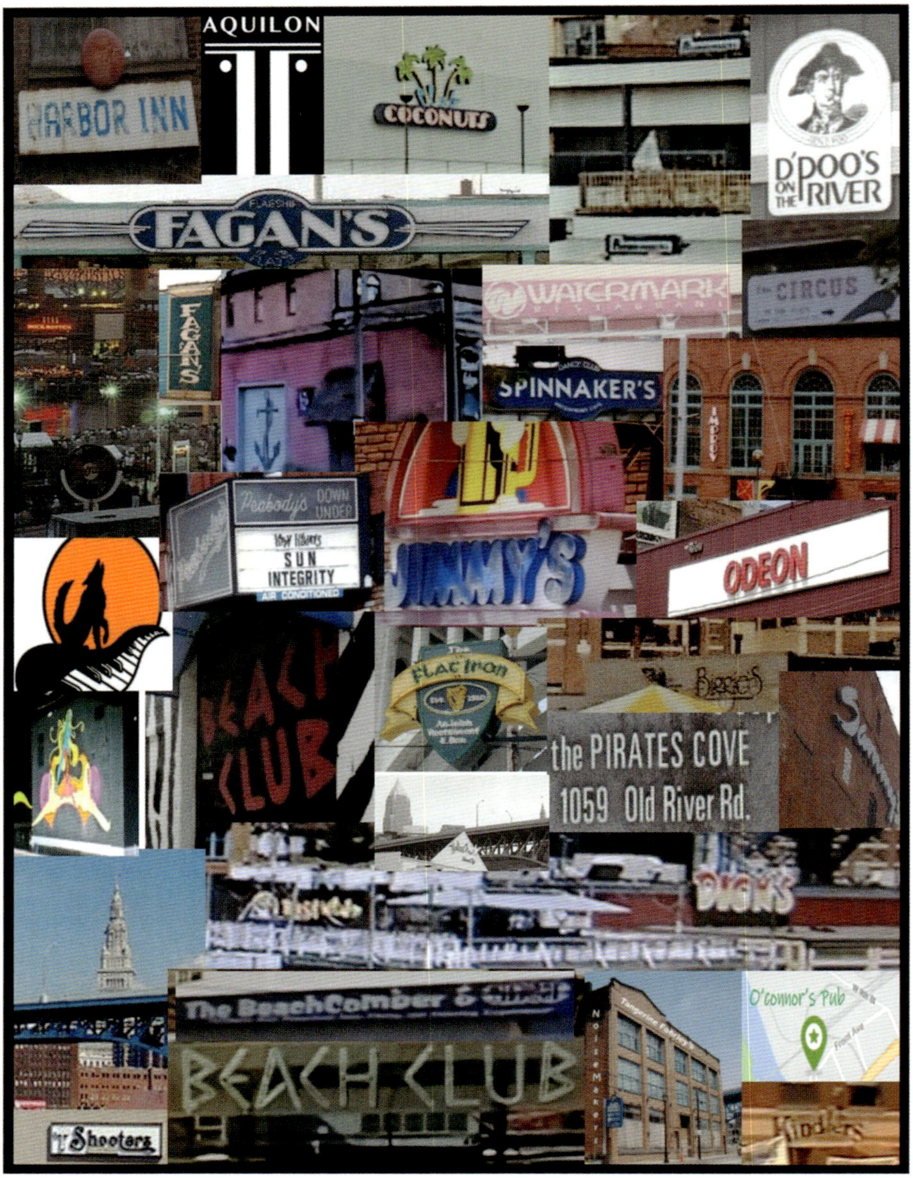

Flats Collage. This fun Cleveland clubs collage, designed by Dolores Resch, gives readers a *Where's Waldo* challenge. It shows the many venue choices Clevelanders had in the Flats during its gritty heyday in the 1970s. The Flats is located on the east and west banks of the Cuyahoga River and has been through more ups and downs than any other area in Cleveland. The region's appeal began to wane in the 1980s, but it enjoyed new life with the opening of riverfront restaurant and bar Shooters on the Water and the building of the Rock Hall. The Flats then had another downslide until recently, when it returned, more glamorous than ever, with bigger, brighter, and newer venues like the Music Box Supper Club. (Designed by Dolores Resch.)

Peabody's/Pirate's Cove. This legendary club began as Peabody's in Cleveland Heights in 1977; however, when it moved to the Flats, it was renamed Pirate's Cove. In 1984, it was rechristened Peabody's Downunder. The venue moved to the Cleveland State campus in 2001 and became Peabody's Concert Club. Despite the name changes, this club enjoyed a popular run, and patrons came to see acts from nearly every musical genre, including mainstream rock, punk, and R&B. In 1982, fans watched a captivating performance by Sam & Dave ("Soul Man"). In 1991, the James Gang reunited after 20 years for a long-anticipated concert at the Nautica Pavilion, using Peabody's for their rehearsals. The venue closed for good in 2013. (Both, photograph by Janet Macoska.)

The Euc. The Mr. Stress Blues Band, led by singer and harp player Bill Miller, played every Saturday night at Euclid Tavern (better known as "The Euc") for more than a decade. Over its 30-year career, the band played nearly every club throughout Northeast Ohio. Miller was a fan favorite, so artist Rick Novario designed this image of the iconic bluesman leaning over an open case of harmonicas. Miller died in 2015. (Courtesy of Rick Novario.)

Euclid Tavern Sign. The Euclid Tavern, one of Cleveland's oldest bars, opened in 1909. However, its heyday didn't come until the late 1970s and '80s, when it became a hotbed for music of all genres and a favorite among the college set. The bright neon sign alerted all to its location on Euclid Avenue in University Circle. Fans got to see Green Day here, as well as Chrissie Hynde. Even rocker Joan Jett and actor Michael J. Fox performed together here for the filming of their 1987 movie, *Light of Day*. The bar became the Happy Dog in 2014 but closed for good in 2018. This sign now resides in Jason Aldean's bar in Nashville.

The Cove Niteclub. Way out in Geneva-on-the-Lake, which is 50 miles east of Cleveland, the Cove Niteclub has been a rock and roll staple since 1963. This venue has a rich history of featuring up-and-coming and established performers from Northeast Ohio and beyond. The fascinating mural along the side of the venue always attracts attention on the strip. The painting, which was created by an unknown artist, pays homage to many of the musicians who have played there through the decades, including the James Gang, Donnie Iris (his band, the Jaggerz, had a hit with "The Rapper"), the Outsiders with Sonny Geraci, Neil Giraldo, and Benjamin Orr, among others. The Cove is alive and well and continues its tradition of showcasing live music. (Both, photograph by Kira Lugo.)

Joan Jett and Michael J. Fox at Phantasy Nightclub. The Phantasy Nightclub, in Lakewood, is another venue with a long history and is known for featuring a number of alternative/underground artists, as well as the unique replica of a 17th-century pirate ship inside the club. In 1987, Phantasy was the site of a rare appearance by Joan Jett and Michael J. Fox on the night before the premiere of their movie *Light of Day* at the Ohio Theatre in Playhouse Square. Former research assistant Grafton Nunes, now president of the Cleveland Institute of Art, recalled in a *Plain Dealer* article that Bruce Springsteen recommended the film be shot (in part) in Cleveland because it has "the greatest rock 'n' roll audience." (Photograph by Janet Macoska.)

Akron Civic Theater. Way down south, about 30 miles from Cleveland, there is a notable venue that has provided entertainment for nearly a century. The esteemed Akron Civic Center offers everything from theater productions and musicals to rock concerts and special events. In 2008, it hosted a Democratic fundraiser, which brought together some notable Akron natives. On hand for the performance were Chris Allen, Rachel Roberts, Chrissie Hynde, and the Black Keys, who opened for DEVO and are pictured here with that group in their iconic gear. (Photograph by Janet Macoska.)

Sunset Harbor Bar & Grille. Summertime is when Clevelanders make up for outdoor hours lost to the colder months. Sunset Harbor Bar & Grille, located in Fairport Harbor on the east side, has a number of amenities. The menu features Lake Erie perch and walleye, and there is an outside tiki bar and a Bloody Mary bar on Sundays. While this seasonal venue has seen its share of blustery storms and ice, which require it remains closed in winter, boaters, bikers, kayakers, pedestrians, and drivers all come to dine on the pier in summer. Owners Tom and Max Moore and Trenda Jones book musical acts and other events all season. Sundays often bring popular duo Poncho & Lefty (pictured below), featuring Brian Lisik (left) and Chad Ely (right), who welcome other players, like James Edwards (center) to join in. With Lake Erie as its backdrop, Sunset Harbor Bar & Grille provides an ideal venue for a perfect day for Clevelanders. (Both, photograph by Aprell Burkey.)

The Odeon. No Cleveland rock book would be complete without including iconic *Plain Dealer* writer Jane Scott. Scott is renowned as the first female rock reporter. In her 50 years of interviewing anyone who was anyone in the rock world, she earned the respect and love of thousands of luminaries. In 1999, when she turned 80 and was still working, her friends held a birthday party for her at the Odeon, located on the east bank of the Flats. Many local musicians who made good performed and credited her for getting their names in print long before their music became well-known. Even the Raspberries reunited for the special event. Jane retired at age 83, and she died in 2011 at age 92. (Photograph by Janet Macoska.)

Coffee Break Concert. The Odeon, with its 1,000-person capacity, was known for showcasing a number of touring acts through the 1990s up until it closed in 2006. Some of the more memorable shows include Nine Inch Nails, the Ramones, Todd Rundgren, Eminem, the White Stripes, and Mushroomhead, who also launched the grand reopening of the Odeon in May 2015. Metallica thrilled fans with a rare Coffee Break Concert for radio station WMMS in 1997. (Photograph by Janet Macoska.)

Five

Blossom Music Center

Blossom Music Center, located in Cuyahoga Falls just north of Akron, is an outdoor amphitheater situated on 200 acres of beautiful rolling hills. Built in 1968 as the summer home of the Cleveland Orchestra, this premier music venue soon became a home for all genres and all ages. The pavilion seats approximately 6,000 people, with space for close to 15,000 on the lawn. Currently, Live Nation runs Blossom Music Center.

The rich, idyllic setting in the grass (the lawn space is general admission) is most popular with the younger set and families, who often bring a picnic basket and sit outside, among the stars, enjoying their favorite sounds. Through the years, Blossom has hosted practically every pop act of its day. It also provided an outlet for those acts whose careers peaked during the 1980s, such as Debbie Gibson, the Cars, Pat Benatar, Billy Idol, and Rick Springfield, and others.

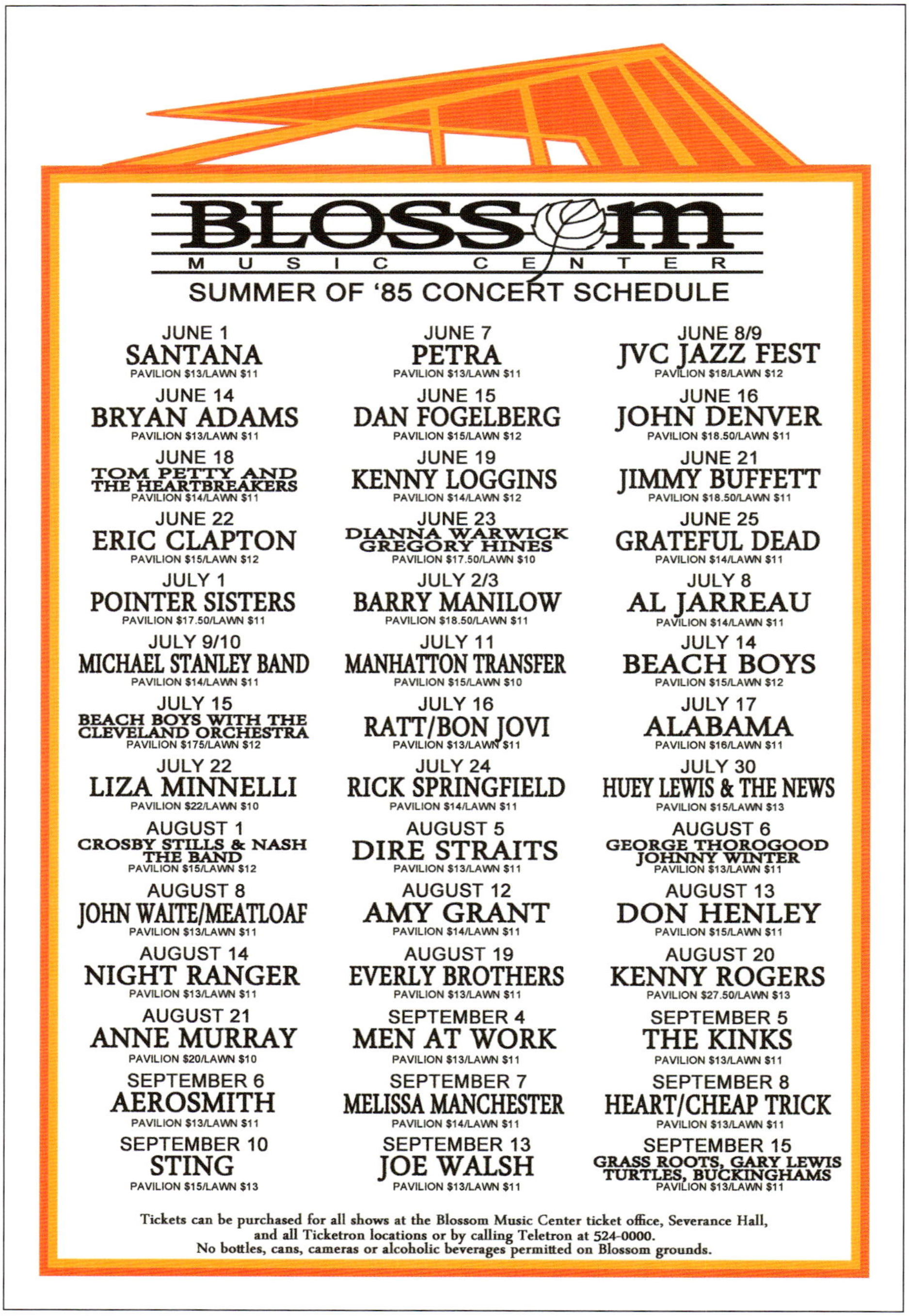

Blossom Music Center Summer of '85 Poster. This lineup demonstrates the wide-ranging events that Blossom has always offered, featuring everything from pop, rock, country, blues, jazz, and special attractions to—of course—the Cleveland Orchestra. In 1985 alone, fans not only had a great choice of acts to see but also could attend shows for prices between $10 (lawn) and $20 (pavilion). (Courtesy of Bear at Raw Sugar Art Studios.)

Michael Stanley Band (MSB) at Blossom. MSB was a Cleveland favorite right from the start. The group toured extensively through the 1980s but received no better welcome than when the hometown heroes played Northeast Ohio. They always sold out the Coliseum and, for their 12-show farewell tour, the Front Row. During the 1980s, MSB headlined at Blossom seventeen times, including four sold-out shows in the summer of 1982 that set a record—with the attendance of 74,404 fans—that has never been broken. "Blossom is a great place," Stanley told the *Akron Beacon Journal*. "It doesn't matter who you go to hear, it's going to be a good musical experience." (Photograph by Janet Macoska.)

Rod Stewart (left) and Bon Jovi (below). Rod Stewart played Blossom Music Center numerous times, always to a full house. Stewart is well familiar with the North Coast, having played at venues in the area since the 1960s, when he performed with the Faces at teen club Hullabaloo. Because of performances like this one at Blossom in 1984, fans never tire of him. Rock band Bon Jovi also came to Cleveland early in its career, in March 1984, to perform a concert at the Cleveland Agora in support of the group's self-titled debut album. A year later, the band was packing stadiums and Blossom Music Center. Bon Jovi was also on hand for the Rock & Roll Hall of Fame's grand-opening concert in 1995. (Both, photograph by Janet Macoska.)

The Bangles (above) and Whitney Houston (right). Girl groups—not just singing groups, but those who play their own instruments—came into their own in the 1980s. Women were not in short supply in the rock world, and Blossom hosted most of them. In 1986, Susanna Hoffs, lead singer of the Bangles, was enjoying the group's rise to the top thanks to their No. 1 singles "Walk Like an Egyptian" and "Manic Monday." That same year, Whitney Houston wowed the crowd with her youthful exuberance and five-octave vocal range. Although she was just starting out at the time, Houston ultimately earned the legacy of being the most-awarded female music artist in history. (Both, photograph by Janet Macoska.)

LINDA RONSTADT. Linda Ronstadt is known for her golden voice and hits such as "Different Drum" (with the Stone Poneys), "You're No Good," and "Heat Wave," which everyone endured at her August 1978 performance at Blossom—one of her many appearances there. Ronstadt sold out two shows as part of her *Living in the USA* tour. (Photograph by Janet Macoska.)

STEVIE NICKS POSTER. The year 1986 brought out the best in female rockers, and Blossom (and fans) embraced the trend. By this time, Stevie Nicks was enjoying a notable solo career that began with her debut solo album, *Bella Donna*. She performed two sold-out shows at Blossom in support of her album *Rock a Little*, which also enjoyed commercial success. In 2019, Nicks was inducted into the Rock & Roll Hall of Fame as a solo act. Because she was already an inductee with Fleetwood Mac, the honor made her the first female artist to be inducted twice. (Courtesy of Bear at Raw Sugar Art Studios.)

Six

BEACHLAND BALLROOM

Beachland Ballroom owners Cindy Barber and Mark Leddy had a vision in 2000 and opened an eclectic music club in a historic building, formerly the Croatian Liberty Home, to pump more life into the old, sleepy neighborhood known as the Collinwood area. The Beachland Ballroom & Tavern, with its weekly musical offerings, sparked a rebirth of the community that is now known for its array of art galleries, record stores, and innovative events. Located on Waterloo Road a half mile south of Lake Erie, Beachland is actually two venues in one. The tavern side is smaller and more intimate, with a 148-person capacity. The ballroom can fit 500—and often does just that. On weekends, the venue offers a Beachland Rockin' Brunch and a deejay spinning vinyl on Sundays. This beloved venue has survived despite some hard times, and the owners, along with Cleveland music fans, look forward to celebrating its 20th anniversary in 2020.

Beachland Signage. Through two decades, an extensive list of rock and roll bands have made their way through the Beachland doors—the building welcomes everyone. There have been legendary performances by the Schwartz Brothers, Pere Ubu, the White Stripes, and the Black Keys. Indeed, this former Croatian hall has always showcased all kinds of music, including polka (the Polka Hall of Fame is just three miles away). It is also a hot spot for burlesque, with sold-out shows several times each year and a three-day festival event every August. Despite the diverse events, it is best known as a home for rock and roll, with most nights featuring two separate local and national shows. (Both, photograph by Jeff Hace.)

Wally and Jesse Bryson. When it comes to showcasing local musicians, the Beachland is the perfect place for Cleveland to honor its own. In 2004, the musical father-and-son team pictured here performed in the ballroom to a thrilled audience. Former Raspberries guitarist Wally Bryson and Jesse Bryson, also a successful musician, formed a duo simply called the Bryson Group. They celebrated the release of their album *Dry* with an exclusive party at the venue, and the recording won critical praise. While Wally Bryson still resides in the Cleveland area, Jesse currently lives in New York City. (Courtesy of Kay Bryson Collection.)

Choir Reunion. Some reunions are more nostalgic than others. This 2018 show brought together one of the area's most beloved bands, the Choir, which had a regional hit (with Wally Bryson), "It's Cold Outside," in 1966. The two sold-out shows celebrated the release of a 1968-recorded Choir album, *Artifact*, thanks to the Los Angeles–based Omnivore Recordings. The five Choir members who played on the album reunited for the Beachland concert. The lineup included original drummer Jim Bonfanti, guitarist Randy Klawon, keyboardists Phil Giallombardo and Ken Margolis, and bassist Denny Carleton. "It's Cold Outside" was written by Klawon's brother Dan when he was just 15. (Photograph by Jeff Hace.)

Adam Blessing Reunion. Another grand reunion that rocked the house occurred when 1960s hard-rock band Damnation of Adam Blessing performed at the Beachland in 2007. This five-piece band was together from 1968 through 1974 and toured for most of that time, playing rock festivals and sharing the stage with bands such as Eric Clapton's Derek and the Dominos, MC5, Grand Funk Railroad, and hometown heroes the James Gang. Despite the passage of more than two decades, the group was welcomed with a full house. (Photograph by Jeffrey Adams.)

Michael Stanley Award. When it came time for the city of Cleveland to honor its "Favorite Son," the Beachland was more than happy to host the party. In May 2019, singer-songwriter Michael Stanley was presented with a Cleveland Arts Prize Lifetime Achievement Award for his 50-year music career, as well as his work in local media and his philanthropic endeavors. Stanley was the cohost of *PM* magazine from 1987 to 1990 and has been the afternoon on-air personality for classic rock station WNCX for nearly 30 years. After the accolades, the party continued with a performance by Michael Stanley & Friends. (Photograph by Joe Kleon.)

Tavern Side. Fans can get up close and personal at the ballroom or the tavern, and jam sessions are perfect for the tavern side. At far left in this image is blues singer/harmonica player "Crazy Marvin" Braxton, who began performing in the 1960s at Leo's Casino. Next to him are, from left to right, sax players Gene Eibler, Brad Stevenson, and Norm Tischler (in red cap). The guitarist at far right is Marc Cvelbar. Cleveland lost a musical icon when Tischler passed away in 2019. (Photograph by Jeff Hace.)

Archie and the Bunkers. Cleveland duo Archie and the Bunkers, which consists of teenage brothers Emmett and Cullen O'Connor, has become known for its organ-driven garage punk sound, which comes from hometown influences like the Electric Eels, the Pagans, the Dead Boys, and Screamin' Jay Hawkins. They have toured the United Kingdom, as well as across the United States, but each time the brothers play their electric "HI-FI Organ punk" in the Beachland Tavern, they add to their homegrown fan base. (Photograph by Kevin McCann.)

Iron Messiah. In 2012, the Beachland held yet another benefit, this time an annual one, featuring heavy metal band Iron Messiah, for the Iron Ingo Cleveland Metal Holiday Food Drive sponsored by college radio station WJCU and event organizer/deejay Bill Peters, whose *Metal on Metal Show* has aired since 1982. This photograph also displays the original vintage details of the building's interior that owners Cindy Barber and Mark Leddy worked to preserve. (Photograph by Joe Kleon.)

Jon Spencer and the HITmakers. For 30 years, singer/guitarist/ composer Jon Spencer has enjoyed a long career with a number of bands (Blues Explosion, Boss Hog, Heavy Trash). Known for his legendary garage/blues/ punk rock, Spencer is also known for some wild vocals and captivating performances. At this 2019 gig at the Beachland, he let no one down. (Photograph by Kevin McCann.)

Seven

Music Box Supper Club

In 2014, to the delight of many who enjoy going downtown for live entertainment, Mike and Colleen Miller opened the Music Box Supper Club, a vibrant two-level venue on the west bank of the Flats. This significant building that once housed Club Coconuts (which is shown in the club collage on page 44) has two stages: the downstairs Supper Club, which includes the Rusty Anchor restaurant, and the upstairs Concert Hall. In five short years, this venue has showcased an array of talent ranging from local and regional musicians to renowned national touring acts. Mike Miller said, "Colleen and I wanted to create a special place to bring people together, and the riverfront location adds to that experience. The Music Box has become a special part of the Northeast Ohio community, and we're always building on the idea."

The venue was named Best Live Music Venue by *Cleveland* magazine readers in 2017 and 2018. The Sunday breakfast brunches that feature musical tributes to Patsy Cline (Rachel and the Beatnik Playboys), the Beatles (Sunrise Jones Band), and many others are a weekly favorite. The Music Box Supper Club is a true gem that highlights the best Cleveland has to offer when it comes to modern music venues.

Outside the Music Box. The Music Box is in the perfect location, with waterfront views whether one sits upstairs or downstairs. The club even has a 24-7 live webcam that shows a bird's-eye view of the Norfolk Southern bridge over the Cuyahoga River, which is especially helpful for the freighters, powerboats, and cruise ships that continually cross Lake Erie to the Flats. The second floor also has a rooftop deck that overlooks downtown. The venue can be rented for weddings, fundraisers, corporate parties, and other events. (Photograph by Joe Milliken.)

Cold Weather, Hot Music. When it comes to entertainment, the Music Box packs the house no matter what the weather. In winter, the venue offers enough appealing weekly events to help prevent Clevelanders from coming down with cabin fever. (Photograph by Ricky Benninger.)

P.J. MORTON AT CONCERT HALL. The Concert Hall of the Music Box is upstairs and has a large stage, high-end sound system, and room for 800 standing or 380 sitting. It has a waterfront view with direct access to the rooftop deck. With these kinds of amenities, a national act like P.J. Morton feels right at home. Morton, an award-winning songwriter, producer, Grammy nominee, and Maroon 5 keyboardist, made Cleveland a stop on his tour in May 2019. (Photograph by Louis Haas.)

CONCERT HALL. Marc Roberge, lead vocalist of O.A.R. (Of a Revolution), is pictured extending a hand to the Music Box sign. Roberge is from Maryland but has been an Ohio fan since his college days at Ohio State University. He and his band have enjoyed a rich career, with Billboard hits like "Shattered" and sold-out shows at Madison Square Garden and Red Rocks Amphitheatre. (Photograph by Steffi Wegewitz.)

SUPPER CLUB. In the restaurant, the Rusty Anchor in the Supper Club level offers a number of popular events through the year on nearly every night of the week. The Cleveland Blues Society (CBS), which hosts a monthly jam night, often makes an appearance at the Music Box. The jam lineups are always different, as is the music. Here, at a 2015 meeting, the players included Bill Mangano and Danny Gerald. CBS member and musician Michael Henighan, who is wearing a checkered shirt and black hat, sits among the appreciative audience. (Photograph by Jeff Hace.)

ALAN GREENE BAND (AGB). Members of the Alan Greene Band are, from left to right, Jason Butcher, bass; T.C. "Odie" Odegard, harmonica and vocals; Rob Luoma, drums; and Alan Greene, guitar. The band is a favorite no matter which venue they play. Here, the group is performing to a full house in the Supper Club. (Photograph by Tammi Hansen.)

Cleveland Storytellers—the Buzzard Crew. The Music Box keeps things interesting even in the coldest of months. Every Wednesday from September through May, the Cleveland Storytellers Series combines education with entertainment in the Rusty Anchor restaurant, bringing area historians, authors, and others to the stage. Mike Miller (at left) leads discussions on topics like local media, pop culture, and even tales of murder and unsolved mysteries. In the image at right, members of the "Buzzard Crew" are shown talking about their careers at radio station WMMS. The panel included former program director John Gorman, newsman Ed "Flash" Ferenc, deejay Denny Sanders, and promotions director John Chaffee. Chaffee wore his original Buzzard T-shirt and is holding a key chain—one of the popular marketing items they used to promote the station. (Photograph by the author.)

Cleveland Storytellers—Deanna R. Adams. Here, Deanna R. Adams, author of this book, tells Mike Miller a humorous anecdote that led her to write her first book, *Rock 'n' Roll and the Cleveland Connection*. (Courtesy of Music Box Supper Club.)

Moving in Stereo. Ever since Cleveland musician Benjamin Orr cofounded the Cars, Cleveland has had a love affair with the group, so it made perfect sense that a band of talented musicians create a tribute to the band. Moving in Stereo performs throughout the state, but Clevelanders get to enjoy them often at the Music Box Supper Club's popular Sunday breakfast brunch, which features a number of performers paying tribute to artists like Patsy Cline, Janis Joplin, the Beatles, and others. Pictured are, from left to right, guitarist Bob Heazlit, drummer Noah Patera, bassist Matt Fuller, Lars Altvater on synthesizer, and guitarist Danny Ayala. (Photograph by John C. Benson.)

The Riverbank. From inside or outside, guests can enjoy the view across the river. Boaters especially love to cross back and forth on the Cuyahoga River so they can hit the clubs on both sides of the Cleveland Flats. Music Box marketing coordinator Ricky Benninger makes a point to capture the sights outside his work environment, appreciating his job through all the seasons. (Photograph by Ricky Benninger.)

Eight

Bars and Guitars

There has never been a shortage of places or musicians to rock in Northeast Ohio. Baby boomers continue to mourn the loss of many clubs, including the Viking Salon, the Corral, Hennessy's, the Barking Spider Tavern, Wilbert's, the Stables, Utopia, Smiling Dog Saloon, and so many others that no longer exist. However, today, there are plenty of venues for anyone to enjoy and keep the city alive with music and fun.

This chapter focuses on venues that continue to thrive, with one exception—the Sahara Club, in Willoughby Hills. Although the club closed in 1991, those who frequented it fondly recall when guitars strummed, whined, and rang through the night at this eastside bar. So, this chapter begins with the famous—or, rather, infamous—Sahara Club.

SAHARA CLUB ADVERTISEMENT. The Sahara Club, located in Willoughby Hills, quickly became the go-to place to hear great live music when owners Jim Cvelbar, David "Tex" Palumbo, and C.C. Buckley Jones opened the club in 1983. When British drummer Jerry Shirley moved to Cleveland in the late '80s, he worked as a Saturday-morning deejay for classic-rock station WNCX and reformed his band Humble Pie with local guitarist Alan Greene. Wild Horses was always a local favorite. As is evident in this ad, the Sahara had something going on nearly every night of the week, and for nearly a decade, no matter who was playing, the club drew an enthusiastic crowd. (Courtesy of Trenda Jones.)

SAHARA. Palm Trees and camels were the theme of the Sahara Club. Here, guitarist Chad Ely, of Mean Idea, plays in front of the iconic camel in 1989. Ely, now president of Ely Multimedia, fondly recalls the venue. "It was a great place to play," he said. "The stage lighting was particularly great, because they had a real spotlight with a working operator, so musicians appreciated that." (Photograph by Anastasia Pantsios; courtesy of Chad Ely.)

East Shore Park, Cebars. When it comes to bars and guitars, members of the Armstrong Bearcat Band and Alan Greene Band have been rocking Northeast Ohio for decades and are still in demand. The above image shows some members of both bands playing at the East Shore Park in Cleveland, which offers a free summer concert series; pictured are, from left to right, bassist Michael Barrick, drummer Billy Coakley, and guitarists Alan Greene, Butch Armstrong, Cy Sulak, and "Neon Don" Buchanan. These veteran musicians have also been a staple at Cebars Tavern. Since 1998, the tavern has hosted jam sessions by the Alan Greene Band on Sunday nights, and on holidays, they have hosted special reunions featuring both bands. These guys are a crowd favorite when they all get down. (Both, photograph by Jeff Hace.)

Hoopples. There is a little blue-collar, working-class bar tucked away in the Flats area that is as unpretentious as an urban watering hole can get. Yet, for those in the know, Major Hoopples is a place Clevelanders go when they seek a simple beer list, good bar burgers, and—with its location on a bluff overlooking the Cuyahoga River—large windows with a sweeping panoramic view of the city. For 20 years, bassist Gene Schwartz (far left) and his brother Glenn Schwartz, a legendary guitarist, played here every Thursday night. Sometimes, guitarist Joe Walsh (right), their longtime friend, would show up to jam with them, as shown in this picture from 1998. (Courtesy of Gene Schwartz Collection.)

Grog Shop and Crowd-Surfing. The Grog Shop opened on Coventry Road (a street rich in pop culture history) in Cleveland Heights in 1992 and traffics in punk, metal, reggae, hip-hop, and indie rock. While the outside view looks unassuming, inside, the club is alive with raw character and offers live music seven days a week, 365 days a year. Kathy Simkoff Blackman has owned Grog Shop since 1992, and it has hosted countless local entertainers, like Carlos Jones & the PLUS Band, as well as national and international touring acts like Bruno Mars, Kid Rock, and Train. It books a wide range indie rock, hip-hop, hardcore, jam, reggae, metal, electronic, and even comedy acts. One never knows what to expect at the Grog Shop. As shown below, Nine Shocks Terror added some crowd-surfing to their 2005 performance. The Grog Shop is currently located at 2785 Euclid Heights Boulevard in Cleveland Heights. (Above, courtesy of Grog Shop; below, photograph by Keith Marlowe.)

House of Swing. Jazz may be king at this South Euclid venue, but it also features its share of rock, and blues. "The House of Swing is a true music bar," owner Linda Kallie, whose late husband was a jazz drummer, told a Cleveland.com reporter. "We don't offer food or give anything away. It's about the music." It is also about the old-time jazz photographs, posters, and the 15,000 LPs housed in it. The collection attracts vinyl lovers, as well as music historians. Note the row of albums lined up behind the band. With a long history on the local scene, the musicians are, from left to right, Tim Matson, guitar; Eva Dilcue, vocals; Joe Alessandro, drums; Don Buchanan, guitar/vocals; and Craig Clasen, bass. (Photograph by Jeff Hace.)

Sly Fox Lounge. The Sly Fox Lounge, a rock club located in North Olmsted, is known for cheap beer, live hard rock, deejays, and cover bands. In 2016, it hosted a party with a poignant theme. For 10 years, Ann Thompson maintained a website, *After the Gig*, that provided the where and when of what was happening at venues across town. In 2016, Thompson decided to hang it up, much to the despair of those who began to rely on the information. But then, it was a good excuse to rock. And the best veteran musicians came out to play. Pictured are, from left to right, Rich Spina, Billy Sullivan, Don Krueger, Bill March, and Cy Sulak. (Photograph by Jeff Hace.)

Hooley House. Another venue that is a regular stomping grounds for residents from all sides of town is the Hooley House Sports Pub & Grille. This Irish American family-owned bar began in Mentor and then branched to several Northeast Ohio markets. They are known for classic Irish dishes and provides live music, ranging from small solo and duo acoustic acts to full-on rock bands, which often pack the house. Here, the Billy Morris Sunset Strip Band performs at the Mentor Hooley. Morris (left) is a Cleveland native who has played in national heavy metal bands, such as Kidd Wicked, Quiet Riot, and Warrant. His current band includes guitarist Rob Samay (right), drummer Ray Brown, and bassist Paul Lewis. (Both, photograph by Jeff Hace.)

FOUNDRY CONCERT CLUB. There is live music happening everywhere one looks in Cleveland. On the west side, the Foundry Concert Club, located in Lakewood, proudly boasts that it is "run by musicians and for musicians." So, the club hosts music ranging from rock to death metal and beyond. Pictured here is veteran drummer Tommy Rich, who has been in a number of bands and is the music director for School of Rock Cleveland. (Photograph by Nancy Yovan.)

FISH BAR. Local Tavern's Fish Bar is located in Painesville, 30 miles east of Cleveland. This bar/restaurant specializes in seafood and music. The club features jam nights on Tuesdays and "Tunes on Thursdays," hosted by musician Kendall Stauffer. Sometimes, a local priest, "Father Tim," stops by to join in. This venue, owned by Tim Roush with partner and head chef John Loxterman, welcomes it all. In this picture taken on the newly built patio, the John Welton & Awakening band, featuring bassist Jono Yowell and keyboardist Ryan Mitiska, is having fun on a summer night in 2019. (Photograph by Kelly Roush.)

Kent Stage Marquee. A little farther south of Cleveland in Kent, Ohio, is a quaint college town with a rich rock heritage that includes musician Joe Walsh. The Kent Stage opened in 1927 and is the sole surviving downtown theater in the county. The venue holds approximately 150 concerts per year, including the Kent Blues Fest and Kent Reggae Fest. With a capacity of just 642 people, the shows often sell out. Each year brings unique offerings, such as David Crosby, the Bacon Brothers, and Billy Bob (Thornton) and the Boxmasters. On a cold St. Patrick's Day in 2019, folks lined up to see Blackberry Smoke. *Rocky Horror Picture Show* fans attended the night before to see a live shadow cast act out the movie. (Photograph by Greg Drugan.)

Diamondback, Elm Street. Lake County, Ohio, east of Cleveland, is one of those places people describe as having "something in the water." Quite a few musicians hail from the area, and many are now hometown veterans who continue to rock the lakeside—and there are always bars, restaurants, and clubs willing to have them. The Diamondback, in Eastlake, which is owned by Moria Fee, offers music on weekends and a jam session on Thursdays with house band Elm Street Blues, which has played steadily for more than 40 years. The group was founded and continues to be organized by brothers Danny (pictured), Chris (not pictured), and Eric (not pictured) McFadden and drummer Hank Hess. The band's newest member is bass player Janet McFadden (pictured), wife of guitarist Danny McFadden. (Photograph by Jeff Hace.)

Billy's. Cleveland music fans are always looking for fun things to do. Some go to a Party in the Park, while others just party in the parking lot. At Billy's Martini Bar in Mentor, as long as there is a live band playing, the people will come, sing along, and dance. The band Sumrada, shown here, is a local favorite, having played nearly every venue throughout Northeast Ohio over the course of more than 25 years—and it has the fan base to prove it. (Photograph by Jeff Hace.)

Nine

Other Notable Venues

Ever since there was a thing called rock and roll, Northeast Ohio has been integrally involved. Eclectic seems like the only proper term to describe the Cleveland-area music scene then and now. The beginning of this book honored the big auditoriums and theaters that welcomed the music and got the rock rolling, followed by notable smaller clubs and bars that made their presence known. Now, toward the end of this history, it's time to come full circle and pay tribute to the other venues, both large and small, that have kept this vibrant city rocking and rolling all day and into the night. This chapter celebrates the old and new places that keep Cleveland alive with music of all genres and for all generations.

House of Blues. The national concert chain House of Blues (HOB), which owns rock-and-blues-themed music venues in markets throughout the United States, opened in the heart of downtown Cleveland in November 2004. As the marquee demonstrates, the club hosts live shows nearly every night of the week, with a variety of musical offerings. Its location is perfect for those who enjoy the music inside but still want to be a part of what is happening outside when the North Coast weather shines. Guests can go early and dine on the outdoor patio thanks to connecting restaurant Crossroads. HOB Cleveland, with a total capacity of 3,000 people, has several areas where patrons can enjoy the performances—the music hall; the restaurant, which features live music on weekends; and the Foundation Room, a VIP lounge. (Left, photograph by Gene Taylor; below, courtesy of House of Blues Cleveland.)

HOB Grand Opening. The House of Blues kicked off in style for its Cleveland opening, when fans got to witness the reunion of beloved 1970s power pop band the Raspberries—with Eric Carmen, Wally Bryson, Jim Bonfanti, and Dave Smalley—after 31 years. The event, pictured above, also featured Billy Sullivan (far left) on guitar; Jennifer Lee on vocals; and Paul Sidoti (far right), who is now a guitarist for Taylor Swift. The sold-out concert led to a new release, *Live at the Sunset Strip*, from the band the following year. In 2005, local country band Lawless took to the HOB stage and filled the house, as shown below. (Above, photograph by Gene Taylor; below, photograph by Janet Macoska.)

Bop Stop. The Bop Stop, located in the near-west side Ohio City, is owned and operated by the Music Settlement, which acquired the club in 2013. The Bop Stop is a truly lovely live music, education, and performance venue and has been hosting regularly scheduled concerts since October 2014. The nightclub atmosphere is alluring, and the venue's location provides a sweeping view of Lake Erie. The acoustically pristine listening room is a blossoming extension of Bop Stop's arts and culture programming and regularly offers music classes for children and adults. While it is best known for jazz concerts, Bop Stop features an array of performances for every musical taste—yet another example of venues existing in all forms. (Both, courtesy of the Bop Stop.)

Brothers Lounge. This venue in Lakewood has a long, rich history dating back to the 1950s. After it closed and went up for sheriff's auction in 2002, co-owners Chris Riemenschneider and Rodger Riggs purchased it, resurrected it, renovated it, and reopened it in 2008. The west side venue now features three rooms: a restaurant/tavern, a cozy wine bar that specializes in acoustic sounds, and the more expansive Music Hall, which hosts rock, blues, jazz, and reggae acts. One night, there could be a country rock band like Ted Riser and the Marshall Band, and another night might feature a father/daughter duo, like when bluesman Colin Dussault and his 12-year-old daughter, Phia, performed together in 2019. Drummer Tommy Amato provided the percussion that evening. (Above, photograph by Jeff Hace; right, photograph by Marc Alu.)

The Winchester. The Winchester Music Tavern, in Lakewood, is another west side venue that offers a mix of entertainment. It opened in 2002 and drew a steady clientele until it closed in 2014, becoming the Bevy in Birdtown. In 2017, Shane Motolik purchased it and has continued its supportive music tradition. Renowned Cleveland musicians Wally Bryson and Rich Spina (keyboardist/bassist and production coordinator for Herman's Hermits, starring Peter Noone) performed at the Winchester in 2012. In 2014, the Winchester welcomed award-winning blues guitarist, singer-songwriter, and inspirational life coach Kelly Richey. (Above, photograph by Nancy Yovan; below, photograph by Jeff Hace.)

Tower City Amp. The former Tower City Amphitheater, later the Time Warner Cable Amphitheater, was an outdoor arena that seated approximately 5,000. It opened to much acclaim in 2001, with scenic views of the city lights and river bridges. The amphitheater hosted about 30 events per year. Due to construction related to the new Horseshoe Casino (now Jack's Casino), it closed in March 2011, but the memories it provided remain in stories and photographs. In 2005, rocker Rick Springfield, best known for his 1981 song "Jessie's Girl," played to a thrilled audience. In 2007, folk-rock duo Indigo Girls enjoyed the sights and breeze as they performed at this venue. (Both, photograph by Janet Macoska.)

Jacob's Pavilion at Nautica. Since it opened in 1987, Jacob's Pavilion at Nautica has been a favorite of many music fans. This 5,000-seat complex is located on the west bank of the Cuyahoga River. It is the largest outdoor-music-only venue in Cleveland and offers a spectacular view of the water with the big-city landscape as a backdrop—Jacob's Pavilion's most unique amenity. At any given time, one can watch as boats of all makes and sizes—especially the giant freighters—navigate through the river, which only adds to fans' delight as they enjoy their favorite performers. Here, Brendon Urie of Panic! At the Disco performs on North Coast in 2014. (Photograph by Janet Macoska.)

Stella's. Stella's Music Club opened in 2018 across from Progressive Field on E. 9th Street. This venue is co-owned and -operated by Megan Savransky, Chris Barone, and Mike Zweig, who named the bar after his favorite pugs. "This is a musician's club," Zweig told *Crain's Cleveland Business*. "Cleveland prides itself as an educated consumer of music, and so, we're excited to learn whether we have satisfied that very high bar in Cleveland." A year in, Stella's Music Club seems to be working. Pictured here is local band Frontier enjoying the new digs. (Photograph by Dan Cornelius.)

Hard Rock Rocksino. The Hard Rock Rocksino, which became MGM Northfield Park in spring 2019, is renowned for its acoustically perfect 1,876-seat concert hall, Center Stage. Located between Akron and Cleveland in northern Summit County, the venue has been Ohio's busiest casino since it opened in December 2013, when Joan Jett kicked off the celebration. The smaller Neon Room hosts comedy acts and local artists with a seating capacity of 300. Cleveland fans spend a lot of time at this venue, especially with annual concerts by Michael Stanley and Donnie Iris and the Cruisers. Although their respective cities (Cleveland and Pittsburgh) are often at odds, Stanley (at left in the image at right) and Iris (at right in the image at right) have been lifelong friends and musical comrades for more than three decades. (Both, photograph by Janet Macoska.)

Mentor Amphitheater. The Greater Cleveland area is home to a number of outdoor venues, including Cain Park in Cleveland Heights; FirstEnergy Stadium, which replaced Cleveland Municipal Stadium in 1999; and Nelson Ledges at Quarry Park in Garrettsville, known for its music festivals. After all, there is nothing quite like enjoying live music in the fresh air. When the Mentor Civic Center began its Mentor Rocks concert series, the venue was round and small but immensely popular, appealing to all generations, as demonstrated when Michael Stanley & Friends played. In 2017, the city built a new, state-of-the-art facility with a 3,000-square-foot stage and twin 14-by-7-foot video screens. Abbey Rodeo performed to a sold-out crowd in 2019. The band includes, from left to right, P.J. Philips, keyboards and vocals; Bob Yocum, guitar, fiddle, and vocals; Verne McClelland, guitar and vocals; Jim Bonfanti, drums and vocals; Chris Butcher, guitar and vocals; and Chuck Citraro, bass and vocals. (Both, photograph by Jeff Hace.)

Ten

Rock & Roll Hall of Fame and Museum

From the day it opened on September 1, 1995, the Rock & Roll Hall of Fame and Museum has been a Cleveland gem, bringing millions of people from all over the world to experience it. Designed by I.M. Pei, the impressive 50,000-square-foot structure, which boasts a triangular glass tent and 165-foot aluminum tower, features a continual rotation of exhibits and special events and has succeeded in shutting down the naysayers while highlighting the city's importance to rock and roll. There are six floors, with each showcasing a multimedia experience and honoring the plentiful genres that have influenced rock and roll: blues, rock, county, and then some. Music enthusiasts will get a good education as they enjoy all the museum has to offer through its permanent exhibitions and traveling national and international shows.

ESTABLISHED IN 1995. It was all about rock and roll on that sunny September 1995 day that brought tens of thousands to the city, as shown above—the event changed Cleveland forever. Before, the city was far down the list of the best places for tourism, but it was ranked in *National Geographic*'s "21 Best Places to Visit" in 2018. The Ohio city came in at No. 14 and was one of only two locations in the continental United States to be listed. Surely, that impressive status has something to do with the Rock & Roll Hall of Fame and Museum. The aesthetics of the building alone, day or night, make it the most photographed landmark in Cleveland. (Above, courtesy of *Plain Dealer* Collection; below, photograph by Janet Macoska.)

2012 Public Hall Inductions. For rock and roll fans, the Rock and Roll Hall of Fame inductions are one of the most anticipated announcements and ceremonious events of the year. While each year brings controversy regarding the artists most deserving of the honor, the chatter quiets down when it comes time to bring the chosen few to Cleveland. In 2012, then-president and CEO, Terry Stewart, stood on stage at the Cleveland Public Auditorium and welcomed the new class, which included Guns N' Roses, Red Hot Chili Peppers, Beastie Boys, Small Faces, Green Day, bluesman Freddie King, Donovan, and others. Throughout the ceremony, fans raise a glass to their favorites. Those without the golden ticket could still enjoy the ceremony down the street, where the Rock Hall rolls out the red carpet for an exclusive simulcast party inside the museum. While there are rumors of another venue hosting the festivities in the future, Rock Hall CEO Greg Harris has said, "We really like having the ceremony at Public Auditorium. [It's] the place where the Beatles played. Where David Bowie first stepped on stage in the U.S. The sense of history at that place is amazing." (Both, photograph by Janet Macoska.)

Bobby Womack. Cleveland native Bobby Womack and his brothers opened for Sam Cooke and the Soul Stirrers at Friendship Baptist Church in Cleveland in 1953. It all began there. Womack went on to have a rewarding career as a soul singer-songwriter and guitarist who also wrote for others. His song "It's All Over Now" became the Rolling Stones' first hit record in the United States. In 2009, Womack finally saw his personal dream come true when he was inducted into the Rock & Roll Hall of Fame. Luckily for him, it happened to be the same year his hometown played host. He greeted fans for a signing of anything they wanted him to sign, including a guitar, before he was led up the escalator to prepare for his performance that night at the Public Hall event. (Both, photograph by the author.)

Jane. Jane Scott has as many fans as any rock star. In 2002, Deanna Adams, author of this book, had her first book launch at the Rock Hall, and ten local artists performed. When it came time for Beau Coup, the group brought legendary *Plain Dealer* writer Jane Scott to the stage to thank her for her years of helping local bands get notable praise and always being kind to them. They then performed a song they wrote just for her, simply called "Jane." (Courtesy of Frank Amato.)

Henke Band. The number of bands that have graced the stage of the Rock Hall is truly impressive and difficult to count. The band shown in this 2011 picture was a bit different than the others; it consisted of Rock Hall employees. Jim Henke (wearing a white shirt), the Rock Hall's chief curator from 1994 until 2012, formed the band, which was appropriately called Exhibit A. It originally had 14 members. Former associate curator Meredith Rutledge-Borger said, "It was a lot of fun." Sadly, Henke passed away in July 2019. (Photograph by Jeff Hace.)

GUITAR MANIA. Throughout the summer of 2007, visitors approaching the Rock Hall saw oversized, wildly painted Fender Stratocaster replicas scattered across the plaza. This was GuitarMania, a greater Cleveland community public art project that raised money for two charities, the United Way of Greater Cleveland and the Rock & Roll Hall of Fame and Museum's educational programs. The guitars were designed by local artists and national celebrities. Many were also displayed throughout the streets of downtown, and today, some are showcased in the terminal and concourse of Cleveland Hopkins International Airport. (Photograph by the author.)

ROCK & ROLL HALL OF FAME AND MUSEUM AT NIGHT. The Rock & Roll Hall of Fame and Museum is perhaps Cleveland's most extraordinary—and most attended—venue. It is much more than a museum. It's an experience, and one that is different for every visitor and with every visit, thanks to the ever-evolving exhibits and events. The Rock Hall's mission has been clear from day one: "To teach, engage and inspire through the power of rock and roll." At the end of a day or night at the Rock Hall, whether visitors spent their time viewing the displays, attending an event, or catching an outdoor concert on the plaza, they walk away with a greater knowledge of rock and roll and an appreciation of where they've been—somewhere special. (Courtesy of Jason Hanley, vice president of education, Rock and Roll Hall of Fame and Museum.)

List of Organizations

The author encourages readers to support the following organizations:

• From the start, the Rock & Roll Hall of Fame and Museum has used its presence not only to entertain but also to educate. The exhibition that opened on July 1, 2019, does exactly that. The Rock Hall's Interactive Garage Exhibit allows guests to play their instrument of choice with trained professionals assisting from on screen. "Most of the changes over the last few years have been to create a more immersive experience for our visitors," Rock Hall president and CEO Greg Harris told Cleveland.com. "When you're talking about rock and roll, nothing gets more immersive than playing actual instruments."

• The Rock & Roll Hall of Fame Library & Archives is the most comprehensive repository of materials related to the history of rock and roll. It is located in a shared building along with the Gill and Tommy LiPuma Center for Creative Arts at the Tri-C Metropolitan Campus, located approximately two miles southeast of the Rock Hall Museum.

• Founded in 1912, the Cleveland Music School Settlement is now known as the Music Settlement. It provides early childhood education, music instruction, and music therapy to people of all ages and levels of experience in northeast Ohio. It is located in Cleveland's University Circle, with a campus in Ohio City and the Bop Stop music and education venue.

• School of Rock Cleveland offers music camps for those of all ages and skill levels, with branches in Westlake, Strongsville, and Highland Heights.